The Little Hands
PlayTime!
Book

WILLIAMSON
Little Hands®

LIBRARY OF CONGRESS CATALOGING-IN-PUBLICATION DATA

Curtis, Regina, 1968–
    The Little Hands playtime! book: 50 activities to encourage cooperation & sharing / Regina Curtis.
        p. cm. — (A Williamson Little Hands book)
    Includes index.
    ISBN 1-885593-42-2
    1. Creative activities and seat work
    2. Cooperation—Study and teaching. I. Title. II. Series.

    LB1027.25 .C87 2000
    372.5—dc21
                                    99-088073

Little Hands® series editor: Susan Williamson
Project editor: Emily Stetson
Illustrations: Elliot Kreloff
Interior design: Pisaza Design Studio, Ltd.
Cover design: Trezzo-Braren Studio
Permissions: Permission to use the following material is granted by Williamson Publishing Company: from *Fun With My 5 Senses* by Sarah A. Williamson: pages 84–85, 86–87, 88–89, 114; *The Little Hands Big Fun Craft Book* by Judy Press: page 19; *Rainy Day Play!* by Nancy Fusco Castaldo: pages 22–23, 25, 41, 83; *Science Play!* by Jill Frankel Hauser: page 49.
Printing: Capital City Press

Williamson Publishing Co.
P.O. Box 185
Charlotte, Vermont 05445
1-800-234-8791

Manufactured in the United States of America

10 9 8 7 6 5 4 3 2 1

Little Hands®, *Kids Can!*®, *Tales Alive!*®, and *Kaleidoscope Kids*® are registered trademarks of Williamson Publishing Company.

Good Times™ and *Quick Starts*™ for Kids! are trademarks of Williamson Publishing Company.

Notice: The information contained in this book is true, complete, and accurate to the best of our knowledge. All recommendations and suggestions are made without any guarantees on the part of the author or Williamson Publishing. The author and publisher disclaim all liability incurred in conjunction with the use of this information. Young children should be supervised by an adult at all times.

Dedication

To my husband, Joe, for his support
and encouragement,
but most of all for his love.

In loving memory of my mother.

Acknowledgments

I would like to thank my friends Lisa Valenzisi and Janean Smith for their help and input; Dave Yellen for his poetic humor; Ralph Valenzisi for just being there; and my little angel Alexa — as you grow, may you always remember the importance of sharing and cooperation.

A special thank you to everyone at Williamson Publishing Company, especially Emily Stetson, whose hard work has helped make this book a dream come true. Thanks also to Diane Downer for her constructive comments, and to illustrator Elliot Kreloff, designers Patricia Isaza and Joe Borzetta, and cover designers Ken Braren and Loretta Trezzo-Braren for their creative talents.

The Little Hands

PlayTime!

Book

50 Activities to Encourage Cooperation & Sharing

Regina Curtis

Illustrations by Elliot Kreloff

WILLIAMSON PUBLISHING • CHARLOTTE, VERMONT

CONTENTS

To the Grown-Ups

During my 10 years of teaching preschool, I have witnessed young children fight over toys, exclude others who are "shy" or "different" from their play, and get frustrated easily by tasks they cannot complete on their own. Sharing, respect for others, asking for and accepting help, and managing anger are not skills that come instinctively to young children. For many children entering preschool, these skills are nonexistent or at best, limited.

Yet, as we are discovering anew every day, these are some of the most important life skills that our children must learn in order to keep our homes, our schools, our communities — and ultimately our kids themselves — safe.

What can we as parents and teachers do to help? Fortunately, plenty! And we can do it in a way that is loads of fun for the kids in our lives. In my teaching, I've discovered that the most effective way to instill cooperation and sharing is to *engage kids in fun activities that encourage them to work together toward a common goal*. Through play, the seeds of sharing, respect, and trust can best be sown and carefully tended.

I wrote *PlayTime!* precisely with this in mind. Each of the creative art projects, crafts, games, and activities is designed to be done with a partner or with a group of kids. While they mix paint colors together to create a new color, form a paper-link friendship chain, or explore feelings in a game of "expression bingo," kids experience the give and take of cooperation, develop a trust of and respect for others, and begin to recognize that we can accomplish things together regardless of our different backgrounds, different abilities, and different points of view. Through cooperative play, children practice crucial social skills that they'll use throughout their lives. Even the simple task of turning on the water after a project for a partner whose hands are messy, or getting a stool to help another kid reach the sink teaches children important lessons of helping and accepting help from others.

This book also recognizes that play is critical to the cognitive and motor development of young children. As children cut, glue, color, draw, and paint in *PlayTime!* activities, they practice *fine motor skills*, while throwing, catching, walking, playacting, and hammering hone their *gross motor abilities*. As kids discuss favorite things, listen to stories, join in conversation, make name art, and dictate or "write" friendly messages, they explore *language and reading*; and through matching, sequencing, counting, and grouping games and activities, they practice *pre-math* concepts. *Science* is part of the fun, too, as kids examine cause-and-effect relationships (Nail-and-String Designs), use their senses (Yum! Butter!), identify and predict (Handprint Colors), and investigate and observe (Colorful Caterpillar). Throughout the book, Helping Hands sections guide parents and teachers to the underlying developmental skills in each activity.

As you explore the fun of play with the kids in your life, always be prepared for the unexpected, including spilled paint and stray glue. Cover work areas with newspaper, use smocks, and add a bit of soap and water to paint to make cleanup easier. Stay relaxed. When children sense that you are uptight about making a mess, they'll be less inclined to express their creativity. And don't worry if an activity doesn't go exactly as planned. Remember that it is the process, not the finished project, that matters. Have fun!

It's PlayTime!

Here you'll find games to play
for many kids or few;
And art created hand in hand
with markers, paint, and glue!

Make bubble art,
create a train;
Try mystery rubbings
and a bowling game!

With another pal print
a spider or tree;
Take a trip with a friend
(it's pretend you'll see!)

Trace a shadow,
play catch with a ball;
Learn to "talk"
with no words at all!

Work together
to get the job done;
With two or more pals
you'll have triple the fun!

Yes, cooperation
is the key to play,
'Cause when kids share together
it's a happy day!

What's Mine Is Yours

(Sharing)

Have you ever wanted to play with a toy that another kid was playing with? Or needed a pal to help you clean up a mess? Imagine how nice it would be if everyone shared with and helped one another. Well, guess what? You can help make that happen!

Bubble Art

Blow some bubbles
and watch them pop,
Then blow some more
with paper on top!

What you need

- Teaspoon
- Dishwashing liquid
- Water
- Large bowl
- Food coloring
- Plastic drinking straws
- Paper

Here we go!

1. With a partner, mix three teaspoons of dishwashing liquid with half a cup of water (125 ml) in the bowl. Add a few drops of food coloring.

2. Place two straws in the bowl.

3. Blow into your straws (don't suck in!), making the bubbles rise up the bowl.

4. Once the bubbles reach the top, place a piece of paper on the bowl. Blow a few more bubbles, so that the paper is covered with bubble prints.

5. Turn the paper over. Write your names.

PlayTime!

Two-Color Bubble Art: Decide with your partner on a different color for a new bubble solution. Blow new bubbles on the same print.

Bubble Wand: Tie a looped string to the end of a stick. Dip the string in the bubble mixture and wave it through the air. Invite others to share in popping them!

Bubble Magic

Be silly with your bubbles! Laugh, "float" with them, and "pop" to the ground in a tumble!

Story Time!
Bubble Trouble by Mary Packard
Just a Bubble Bath by Mercer Mayer

Clay Play

Add a color to clay;
any one will do.
Is it red
or green or blue?

What you need

- Large bowl
- Play Clay*
- Food coloring

* Play Clay: 2 parts flour, 1 part salt, 1 part or more of water (enough to make a dough)

Here we go!

1. In a large bowl, make the Play Clay. Divide the clay and share it with a partner.

2. Press a finger into the clay, making a small hole in each piece.

3. Place a few drops of food coloring* — your choice of color — into each hole. (Do this part alone, so that no one else sees what color you pick.) Close up the hole.

4. Trade clay with a partner. Play with your new clay. Watch to see what color it turns!

 **Story Time!**

Is It Red? Is It Yellow? Is It Blue? by Tana Hoban
Color Dance by Ann Jonas
Purple, Green and Yellow by Robert Munsch

 **PlayTime!**

Scented Clay: Instead of food coloring, place different scented items into the hole (cocoa powder, instant coffee, cinnamon). Now, trade clay with someone else. Use your smelling powers to figure out the hidden scents.

*Tip: Undiluted food coloring stains easily. Protect clothes with a smock.

 **Helping Hands**

Extend the sharing aspect of art activities by encouraging cooperation during cleanup, too. Providing choices invites cooperation: "Do you want to wipe the table or put the supplies away?" If a child is unwilling to help, acknowledge the other participant: "Chelsea, you did a great job cleaning up. Thank you." The nonparticipant will notice.

Dot to Dot

Bird

by Tommy and Megan

A bunch of dots,
what shall they be?
Connect them first
and then you'll see!

What you need

- Paper
- Markers and crayons

Here we go!

1. Draw dots on a piece of paper.
2. Give your dotted paper to another kid to connect the dots to make a picture or design.
3. Label the picture with a title and both of your names.
4. Make another picture together, with your partner making the dots and you connecting them.

Story Time! *Ten Black Dots* by Donald Crews
Dots, Spots, Speckles, and Stripes by Tana Hoban
Draw Me a Star by Eric Carle

Star Pictures

Have you ever looked at the night sky with a grown-up? The glittering stars are like giant dot-to-dot pictures.

People through the ages have used their imaginations to connect stars into pictures called *constellations*. Ask a grown-up to show you the Big Dipper and the Little Dipper. They are two of the most famous constellations.

Make your own constellations by dripping dots of glue on dark construction paper. Sprinkle with glitter. Connect the glitter dots with white chalk to make a special constellation picture. Tape it to your ceiling and look at it when you're in bed at night!

Helping Hands

The dilemma for the kids is that they each will see different images in the dots. Model for kids how to *listen* (to their partners), *look* (at the picture with the explanation), and *react* (acknowledge what the partner says). Then, they can describe what they see. Emphasize that there is no right or wrong — just two different ideas.

Handprint Trees

Arms in paint,
fingers, too;
Sharing art
is fun to do!

What you need

- Tempera paints (brown, green, orange, red, yellow, and white), in dishes or lids
- Paintbrushes
- Paper
- Glitter (optional)
- Markers

Here we go!

1. Paint the underside of a partner's arm and hand with brown paint.

2. Let your partner make the first arm-and-hand print on the paper to create a tree's trunk and branches.

3. Have your partner paint *your* arm and hand. Print a second tree-trunk picture.

4. Make two more tree pictures, so that you have four. Let pictures dry.

5. Sharing pictures, work together to add fingerprint leaves. How will you show the different seasons? Try adding some thumbprint apples!

6. Mount the pictures on a large sheet of paper. With grown-up help, write the season underneath each picture in big letters.

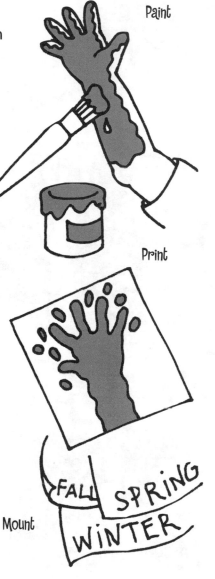

Paint

Print

Mount

FALL SPRING WINTER

Story Time! *The Seasons of Arnold's Apple Tree* by Gail Gibbons
Look at a Tree by Eileen Curran

PlayTime!

Quick Draw: Draw pictures of something you each like to do in your favorite season, and then guess each other's favorite season.

Nature Explore: Take a nature walk with a grown-up. Look for animals and insects; examine how the trees are "dressed" for the season. Can you tell the season from your observations? For a clue, look at how you are dressed, too!

Tip: Use a dark-colored paper for the winter tree picture, so that white paint will show up better. Add glitter to the wet paint to make "snow."

Helping Hands

Here the challenge is for kids to recognize what is fun (painting another person) and what is mean-spirited (not stopping when your partner says, "That's enough paint"). Guide kids to recognize the limits of fun: "Maya doesn't seem to want her arm painted." It's all part of the balance of cooperative play.

Picture Puzzles

A puzzle ...
what can it be?
Put it together
so you can see!

What you need

- Crayons and markers
- White construction paper
- Child safety scissors
- Large envelope

Here we go!

1. Color a picture or design on the construction paper, filling up the whole paper.
2. Cut the paper into a few large puzzle pieces. Put all the pieces in an envelope.
3. Trade puzzles with a partner.
4. Try out your new puzzle!

Tip: Cut the picture into only a few large pieces to avoid frustration.

Personal Puzzle: Try the same idea using an enlarged photocopied picture of you. Glue the picture to construction paper; then, cut it into pieces. Now, put it back together.

Backward Puzzle: Ask a grown-up to cut a large piece of white paper or poster board into puzzle shapes. Work together with several other kids to piece the puzzle back together, and use masking tape to hold the pieces together. Turn the puzzle over. Decide together on a theme for your puzzle, and then draw the picture.

Helping Hands

Teach basic puzzle-solving strategies: Separate the pieces into alike groups. Find all the corner pieces, and the pieces with straight sides. Then, separate the remaining pieces into groups of similar colors or patterns.

Raindrop Painting

Pitter, patter ...
what makes that sound?
Rain on the roof,
dripping to the ground.

What you need

- White paper
- Newspaper
- Aluminum pie tins (one per color)
- Tempera paints, watered down slightly
- Paintbrush

Here we go!

1. Place the paper on newspaper.

2. Ask a grown-up to poke small holes in the pie tin. Hold the pie tin above the paper while a partner pours a small amount of paint into it.

3. While the pourer pushes the paint through the holes with the paintbrush, move the tin around above the paper, making a colorful rainy day design. Hold the pie tin at different heights above the paper to experiment with the design.

4. Switch roles, and use different colors to complete your shared "raindrop" picture.

Hold & pour

Experiment!

 Story Time!

It Looked Like Spilt Milk by Charles G. Shaw
Just a Rainy Day by Mercer Mayer
Rain by Peter Spier

Rain Stick

Soft rain
on dirt and sand,
For thirsty plants
from land to land.

- Safety glasses
- Thick cardboard tube (the type posters are sent in)
- Hammer or wooden mallet
- Flat-headed nails
- Masking tape
- Dried beans or rice, 1/2 cup (125 ml)
- Tempera paint, in dishes or lids
- Paintbrushes

Here we go!

1. Put on safety glasses. One child (or a grown-up) holds the cardboard tube in place, while the other hammers some nails into the side.
2. Take turns hammering and holding until you have as many nails in the tube as you'd like.
3. Wrap masking tape around the tube to keep the nails from falling back out.
4. Close one end of the tube with masking tape.
5. Take turns pouring the dried beans or rice into the other end of the tube. Close the tube with masking tape.
6. Paint and decorate the tube. Then, share the sound it makes with others!

Bringing the Rain

Authentic rain sticks, made by native peoples of the Americas and Africa, were often made from the dried branches of desert plants, decorated with beautiful designs.

Tip: Use nails with large heads. The more nails that are hammered in, the prettier the sound.

Note: Close grown-up supervision (and help as needed) is required at all times.

Rain Talk by Mary Serfozo
The Rainstick: A Fable by Sandra Chisholm Robinson
Rain by Robert Kalan
Bringing the Rain to Kapiti Plain by Verna Aardema

Story Time!

Helping Hands

Working with nails and a hammer can be a wonderful cooperative and trust-building experience for young children (plus it's great for practicing eye-hand coordination). Children may hit their fingers a few times, but they won't seriously hurt themselves.

Spider Print

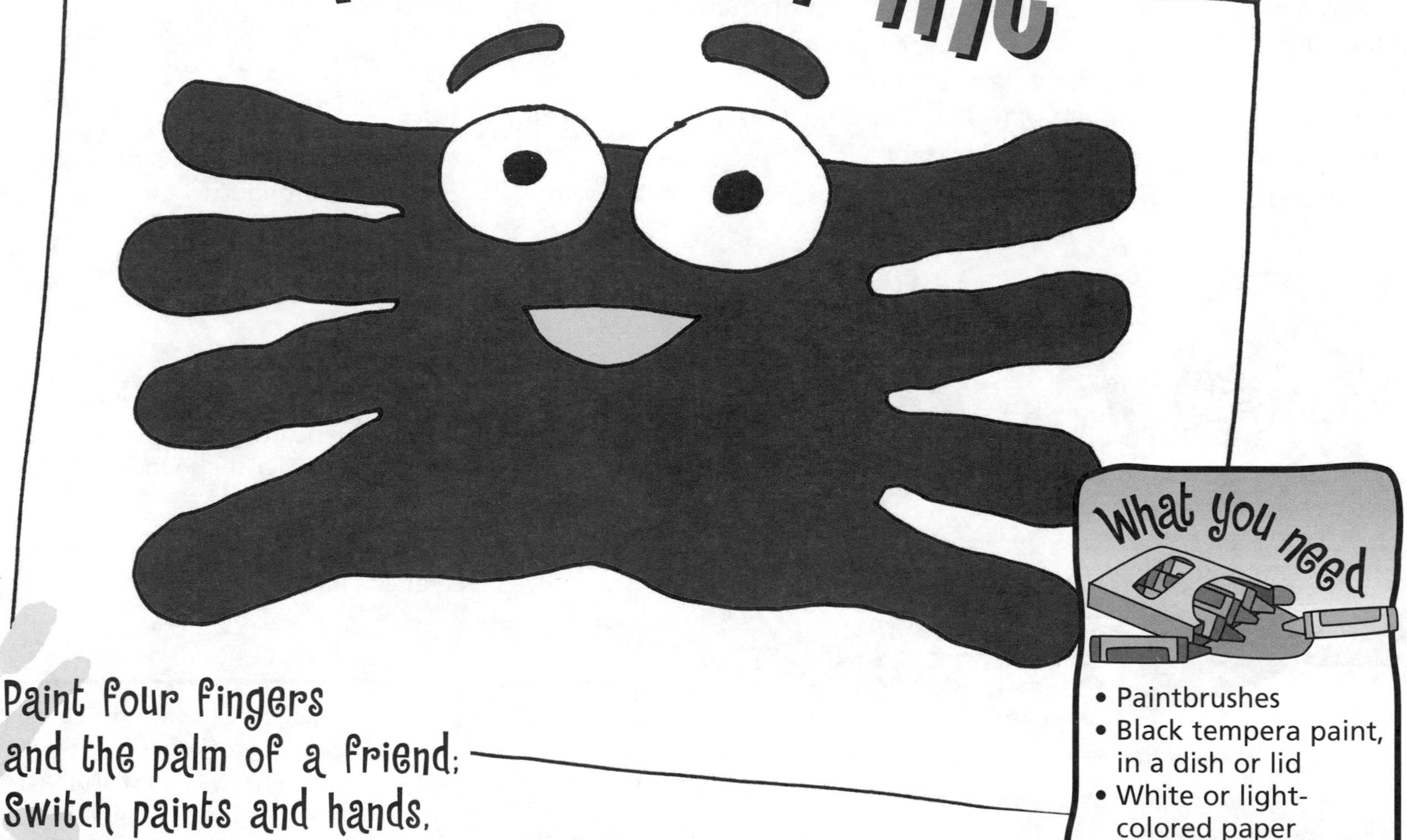

Paint four fingers
and the palm of a friend;
Switch paints and hands,
and do it again.

What you need

- Paintbrushes
- Black tempera paint, in a dish or lid
- White or light-colored paper
- Scrap paper
- Child safety scissors
- Glue

Here we go!

1. With a paintbrush, cover one of your partner's hands with black paint, coating the palm and fingers, but not the thumb.

2. Have your partner make a handprint on the paper.

3. Repeat steps 1 and 2, switching roles. Make the second handprint on top of the first handprint, palm over palm, so that the fingers face out in the opposite direction. Let paint dry.

4. Cut out paper eyes and glue them onto your shared spider.

Paint

Print

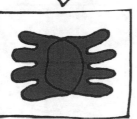

Spider Web Toss

Sit in a large circle on the floor with a group of kids. One player, the first "spider," holds a large ball of yarn. While holding tightly to one end of the yarn, the "spider" rolls or lightly tosses the ball to someone else.

As the "spider" tosses the yarn, she calls out a compliment to the new "spider" ("I love Sami's red hair!"). The new "spider" throws the yarn ball to another new "spider," and the web continues until everyone is holding a piece of the yarn and has had a turn being the "spider." What a wonderful web you've made together!

The Very Busy Spider by Eric Carle
Itsy Bitsy Spider by Iza Trapani
Anansi the Spider: A Tale from the Ashanti
  by Gerald McDermott

Sharing Quilt

Squares of fabric
colored bright,
Sewn together
make a quilt just right!

What you need

- Small squares of fabric, 6" x 6" (15 x 15 cm), 4 per child
- Fabric paint, various colors
- Fabric glue

Here we go!

1. Decorate four squares of fabric with fabric paint. Let the paint dry overnight.
2. Trade two or three of your quilt squares with other kids.
3. Glue the four squares together, or have a grown-up sew them together, to make a four-square quilt.

Decorate

Glue or sew

PlayTime!

Paper-People Quilt: Draw four self-portraits on paper. Trade portraits with others so that you have portraits from four different people. Glue the edges of the pictures together to make a quilt.

So Special: Do you have a blanket or toy at home that has a special meaning or was made by someone just for you? Share its story with others, telling why it is so special to you.

Story Time!

The Quilt Story by Tony Johnston
The Josefina Story Quilt by Eleanor Coerr
The Keeping Quilt by Patricia Polacco
The Quiltmaker's Gift by Jeff Brumbeau

Helping Hands

Some children are reluctant to share personal stories in a group. Don't force the issue, but when you see a spark of interest, invite participation without seeking personal disclosure.

Leaf Batik

Trees tall,
leaves fall,
yellows and reds,
on our heads!

What you need

- Newly fallen leaves
- Muslin cloth
- Cereal-box cardboard
- Wooden mallet

Here we go!

1. Collect newly fallen leaves with a partner.
2. Place a piece of muslin over the cardboard.
3. Arrange the leaves on top of the muslin.
4. Take turns hammering the leaves on top of the muslin.
5. Remove the leaves. What colors and patterns are left on the cloth?

Tip: Can't find a wooden mallet? Try using a piece of wood as a hammer.

Story Time!

Red Leaf, Yellow Leaf by Lois Ehlert
Why Do Leaves Change Color? by Betsy Maestro
Frog and Toad Are Friends by Arnold Lobel

PlayTime!

Leaf Catchers: Outside with a partner, hold a sheet or a piece of contact paper (sticky side up) between you. What can you capture — petals, blossoms, nuts, or the leaves as they fall from trees? Working together, move the sheet around to catch the falling objects.

Join the Fun: Each season has its own special activities, and they're even more fun to do when you share them. Fly a kite in the spring, buddy up for a bubble-blowing blast in the summer, pick apples together in the fall, or make snow angels together in the winter. Share the fun with others, any time of year!

Helping Hands

Encouraging young children to play (and work) cooperatively and to take turns are ways to develop sharing skills. By introducing children to sharing by participating in a common *activity*, rather than struggling with the sharing of an *object*, you help children experience the fun of working together to accomplish a common goal.

Yum! Butter!

Make your own butter
(as kids did some years back),
Then, share it with others
for an extra-special snack.

What you need

- A clean, empty small jar with lid
- Heavy cream
- Saucer
- Spoon
- Crackers

Here we go!

1. Fill the jar halfway with heavy cream. Cover tightly.

2. Take turns shaking the jar, until you see a lump of soft butter form at the bottom. (Arms getting tired? It's lucky you have others to share the shaking!)

3. Pour off the leftover liquid and place the butter in a saucer. Press the butter with the back of the spoon, squeezing out more water.

4. Spread the butter on crackers and share it together. Yum!

SHAKE

YUM!

Story Time! *I Am Sharing* by Mercer Mayer

PlayTime!

Share a Treat: Spread your homemade butter on toast and top with your favorite jam. Share it with a pal, or a favorite stuffed animal.

Helping Hands

This activity provides a wonderful opportunity to show the benefits of cooperation. Taking turns helps those sore arms, and working together yields a totally new treat — butter from cream! Encourage a shy participant by highlighting his contribution: "I noticed Jordan really shaking the jar."

Fun With Friends

(Respect and Trust)

Your friends may be old or young, and live close by or far away. Some friends might know you just a little, and others might know you really well. What friends all share, though, is respect and trust. Friends care!

Have fun with the friends around you — new and old — as you discover what it means to be a friend to others.

To Make a Friend, Just Be a Friend

- Play with a new kid at school. Sit together at snack time, or do a craft project together. Just smiling at someone new is a great way to start!

- Invite someone sitting alone at lunch to join your table. That's always a nice thing to do!

- Has someone missed a lot of school? Call him up to say, "Hi!"

- Ask permission to invite someone you haven't played with before over to your house.

- With a grown-up, make plans to visit an older neighbor. You could even have a tea party together, with homemade cookies you bake ahead of time.

- No one around to play with? Pets, stuffed animals, and books can be your friends, too!

Story Time!

That's What a Friend Is by P. K. Hallinan
How to Be a Friend by Laurie Krasny Brown
George and Martha: The Complete Stories of Two Best Friends by James Marshall
Frog and Toad by Arnold Lobel

Friendship Chain

One link, two links,
three links, four;
Lots of kids
help the chain grow more!

What you need

- Glue
- Construction paper
  in assorted colors,
  cut in 1" x 8"
  (2.5 x 20 - cm) strips

Here we go!

1. Glue the ends of one paper strip together to make a chain link.

2. Ask a partner to put another strip of paper through the first link, and glue the ends to make a second link.

3. Keep taking turns adding to the paper chain. How long is the friendship chain now? Wow! Do each of you want to take another turn?

Tip: Hold the paper tight where glued for a count of 10 before adding the next link.

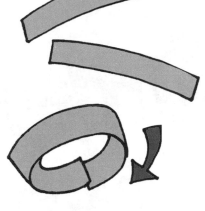

PlayTime!

Kid Links: Make your own long paper chain. Then, join it together with a partner's paper chain, and those of other children until every kid's chain is included. How long is your chain now? Hang your group chain across the ceiling.

Photo Links: Tape a small photo of each person on a link. Then, join the links to make a friendship photo chain.

Pattern Fun: Make the paper chain in a repeating pattern of colors: red-blue-yellow, red-blue-yellow, and so on.

Story Time!

A Weekend with Wendell by Kevin Henkes
Friends by Helme Heine
Horace and Morris But Mostly Dolores by James Howe

Helping Hands

Here kids interact by becoming part of the larger "chain." Along with enhancing social skills, this activity focuses on fine motor skills and eye-hand coordination. If a child is having difficulty, pair an older mentor with a younger partner, and model respect for all levels of ability.

Tulip Garden

Flowers blossom,
friendships, too.
Make a garden
two by two!

Here we go!

1. You and a partner each dip your pointer fingers in green paint. Make stem lines down the paper.*
2. Paint palms and fingers green, and add handprint leaves to each stem.
3. For flowers, take turns making side-by-side handprints in bright colors at the top of each stem.
4. Make a sign for your garden at the bottom of the picture to show which two kids made the garden!

*Tip: The flowers take up quite a bit of room. Place stems several inches apart and leave room at the top to allow enough space for leaves and flowers.

PlayTime!

Rhyming Fun: Say the Mother Goose rhyme "Mary, Mary, Quite Contrary" with a partner. Then, one of you asks the question, "Mary, Mary, quite contrary, how does your garden grow?" The other answers, "With silver bells and cockle shells, and pretty maids all in a row." Take turns with lots of rhymes and songs.

Story Time!

Harriet and the Garden by Nancy Carlstrom
Planting a Rainbow by Lois Ehlert

Helping Hands

This activity works equally well as a larger group activity where everyone becomes part of a flower on a big piece of butcher paper. Each child writes his name next to his print. In a smaller or paired grouping, simple tasks such as deciding where the flower stems will go and which colors to use help kids develop a respect for another's ideas. Pair children with differing backgrounds and personalities whenever possible to cultivate acceptance of differences.

What's Growing?

Trust, respect, and loyalty
make a friendship bloom.
Like tiny seeds that sprout and grow
in a sunny room.

What you need

- Paper cups or pint-sized milk cartons
- Colored tissue paper
- Glue
- Planting mix
- Seeds (sunflowers, beans, marigolds, or peas)

Here we go!

1. Decorate the outside of the paper cup or milk carton with colored tissue paper.

2. Fill the container with planting mix. Plant easy-to-grow vegetable or flower seeds (two seeds of the same type) without anyone else seeing.

3. Water your seeds, and then trade mystery plants with another kid. Important: Don't tell what kind of seed you planted! Let it be a surprise.

4. Put the containers in a bright spot, such as a sunny windowsill, and watch what grows!

Tip: Choose big seeds that are easy to plant and are sure to sprout!

 **Story Time!**

The Carrot Seed by Ruth Krauss
Tops & Bottoms adapted by Janet Stevens

 **Helping Hands**

To help kids communicate, each child reports back to her "planter," using observations to predict what it is. ("I see pink, so I think it is a flower.") Encourage respectful responses ("Good guess!" not "Nope, that's not what I planted!"). Model how to address a person: Look at the person to whom you are speaking.

Friendship Necklace

Something special
to keep close at heart;
For friends to share
when they're apart!

What you need

- Play Clay (see recipe, page 4)
- Rolling pin
- Small paper cup
- Plastic knife
- Plastic drinking straw
- Paintbrushes
- Tempera paints, various colors, in dishes or lids
- Yarn

Here we go!

1. Roll or pat clay flat. Use the rim of the cup to cut out a clay circle.

2. Divide the circle of clay in half. Use the straw to poke a hole through the top of each half-circle of clay.

3. Let the Play Clay air-dry for a few days, or ask a grown-up to place it in an oven set at 200°F (90° to 100°C) for one to two hours.

4. Paint one half of the dried clay. Ask a partner to paint the other half. Let dry.

5. Thread yarn through the holes to make two necklaces. Then, trade necklaces. Each of you now has one half of the friendship circle!

Cut out

Divide

Poke

PlayTime!

Colorful Paper Beads: Cut out 1/2" x 5" (1 x 12.5 cm) strips of colored paper. Wrap the strips tightly around a pencil. Glue the end down so the paper doesn't unravel (hold the paper firmly for about 10 seconds to dry). Slide your colorful beads off the pencil; string for a necklace.

GLUE

Helping Hands

Adults can't force friendships. However, there are steps you can take to help shy children interact more easily with others.

- Pair up kids who you think might enjoy being together.
- Give a special project to "loners."
- Model friendly behavior.
- Correct poor social skills in private.
- Find another student to mentor a younger one, giving one-to-one practice.
- Never have kids choose teammates, pick partners, or "switch" partners.

Wreath of Friends

Your circle of friends
from many lands
Will grow like this wreath
if you lend a hand!

What you need

- Paintbrushes
- Tempera paints, many colors, in dishes or lids
- Square of light-colored fabric, felt, or paper
- Glue
- Glitter, bows, or other decorations
- Wooden dowel
- String or yarn for hanging

Here we go!

1. Paint the palm and fingers of one hand.

2. Taking turns, place your painted hands onto the cloth or paper in a circle, to make a wreath of handprints. Let the paint dry.

3. Glue on glitter, bows, or other decorations. When complete, wrap the top of the cloth or paper around the dowel and glue edges down. Add yarn or string to the ends of the dowel so that you can hang the wreath.

4. Ask a grown-up to write the names of each wreath-maker in the center of the wreath.

Celebrate individuality! Let each child choose his favorite color for his print.

PlayTime!

Circle Play: Stand together in a circle, with one child in the middle. The circle asks, "What can you do, Punchenella, Punchenella? What can you do, Punchenella from the zoo?"

The child inside the circle starts an action (clapping hands, hopping, tapping head), and the others copy her, saying, "We can do it too, Punchenella, Punchenella. We can do it too, Punchenella from the zoo!" Play until every person who wants to has had a turn being Punchenella.

Story Time! *All the Colors of the Earth* by Sheila Hamanaka
Together by George Ella Lyon

Helping Hands

As children make handprints, invite them to discuss how their hands are alike (they all have five fingers and can make a clapping sound) and different (sizes, colors, scratches, freckles). Then, join hands in a circle, and hold arms and hands high in a cheer to celebrate being together!

If a child is too shy to be in the center of a game such as Punchenella, encourage other participation: "Josh, you're doing such a great job jumping!"

Games Galore!

Annie eats almonds and likes animals!

New friends,
new names;
Sharing laughter,
playing games.

Name Game

Sit in a circle. One child starts off by saying her name, followed by a describing sentence (it can be silly or true) that includes words with the same beginning sound as her name: "Annie eats almonds and likes animals." The next person repeats the sentence, and adds another one that uses his name: "Annie eats almonds and likes animals. Ian loves ice cream and icicles." Continue around the circle, until everyone has added a name sentence. Can you still remember the first sentence? Help each other out if you get stuck!

Silly Changing Floor

Spread out pieces of paper on the floor, one per kid, not counting the leader. Everyone walks around the floor, making sure not to touch the pieces of paper. When the leader calls out, "Flood coming, jump on a rock!" all players jump onto a piece of paper. When the leader calls, "Rocks are quicksand!" you jump off your paper. Continue playing, changing the floor and paper into different things. Take turns being the leader.

FLOOD COMING!

Helping Hands

Respect and trust in game-playing are the bases for good sportsmanship. Choose cooperative games that include all participants equally whenever possible. When team games are played, focus on the value of working well together, valuing each player, rather than the score of the game. Model respectful behavior of all kids' abilities.

Hula-Hoop Basketball

You'll need a hula hoop or bucket, a bean-bag ball or toy, and a partner to play this game. Hold the hula hoop in front of your body like a basketball hoop. Have the partner throw the bean bag through the hoop or into the bucket to make a basket. Switch roles, so that you become the thrower and your partner is the holder.

Friendly Sit-Ups and Stand-Ups

These exercises require teamwork!

Stand-Ups: Sit on the floor back to back with a partner. Interlock arms, and bend knees. Now, try to stand up together!

Sit-Ups: Lie on a carpet or a mat on your back with your knees sticking up and your hands clasped behind your head. Ask a partner to hold your ankles down so your feet stay on the floor. Try some sit-ups, slightly lifting your head. Can you do five sit-ups, or maybe even 10? Count them out. Then switch roles, so that you hold your partner's feet for a round of sit-ups.

Story Time! *Will I Have a Friend?* by Miriam Cohen
Amos & Boris by William Steig

Just the Two of Us

(Cooperative Play in Pairs)

Have you ever noticed that when you're playing with a partner, you often come up with lots more ideas of what to do? With another person around, you have someone to talk with, someone to help you, someone to share in the imagining and the decisions — and someone to add to the noise and laughter! Yes, with two of you playing together, there's sure to be double the fun!

Handprint Colors

One hand yellow, another, blue —
the first is mine; the other's from you.
Put them together and what do you see?
A whole new color, made by you and me!

What you need

- Paintbrushes
- Tempera paints, primary colors (red, blue, yellow), in dishes or lids
- Big sheets of paper

Here we go!

1. Paint your partner's hand one color. Have your partner paint your hand another color.

2. Each of you makes one handprint on the paper. Name the colors you printed.

3. Reapply the paint. Rub your painted hand with your partner's painted hand, mixing the colors.

4. Make two new handprints with the new color you created together.

5. Name the new color. How did the two of you together make a new color you didn't have before?

GREEN
by RACHEL + TOM

RACHEL: BLUE   TOM: YELLOW

There's a surprise in store, but it will take a magical ingredient: cooperation!

PlayTime!

Sharing Colors: Sit across from a partner at a table, with a piece of paper between you. Squirt a glob of red, blue, or yellow paint on the paper. Mix your paints to make new colors. Together, make a picture on the paper.

Color Alert! How many colors can you count when you look around you? Five? Maybe 10? There are actually hundreds of different colors — all the colors in your crayon box — and lots more! But all of these colors begin with just three basic colors: red, yellow, and blue. Wow! What a colorful world we live in!

Story Time!

Little Blue and Little Yellow by Leo Lionni
Mouse Paint by Ellen Stoll Walsh
Colors Everywhere by Tana Hoban

Helping Hands

Encourage children to *predict* what will happen when the colors are mixed. Point out the cooperation involved: "By working together, Rachel and Tommy made green."

This is a good activity for pairing children of different temperaments — a shy child and a more dominant child, for example.

Silly Upside-Down Art

Markers below,
paper up high;
upside-down art
is fun to try!

What you need

• Masking tape
• Butcher paper
• Crayons and markers

Here we go!

1. Tape a large piece of butcher paper to the underside of a table.
2. You and a partner lie down under the table on your backs.
3. Together, plan and color a picture on the paper.

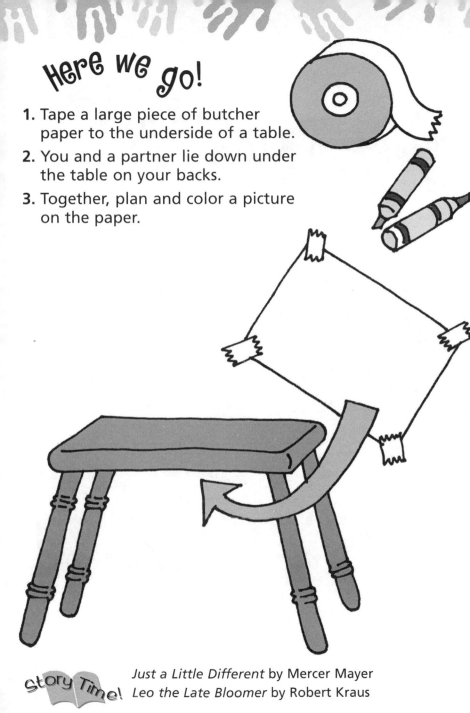

Story Time! *Just a Little Different* by Mercer Mayer
Leo the Late Bloomer by Robert Kraus

PlayTime!

Gigantic Jacket: Ask a grown-up to put a grown-up-size jacket on you and a partner — one sleeve for your arm, and one sleeve for your partner's arm. How will you zip or button up the jacket? Can you both sit in one chair? What about getting a drink from a faucet? See what you can do together. Remember to move very slowly!

Helping Hands

This is a fun way to invite kids to cooperate and it introduces the concept of different ways of doing things. If children can't reach the paper under the table by lying down, add pillows or have them sit up. To increase the challenge, tie one arm from each child together. Ask them to make the picture using their "super" arm.

Nail-and-String Designs

Hammer like a carpenter
(watch your thumb!);
A partner adds the string,
and the design is done!

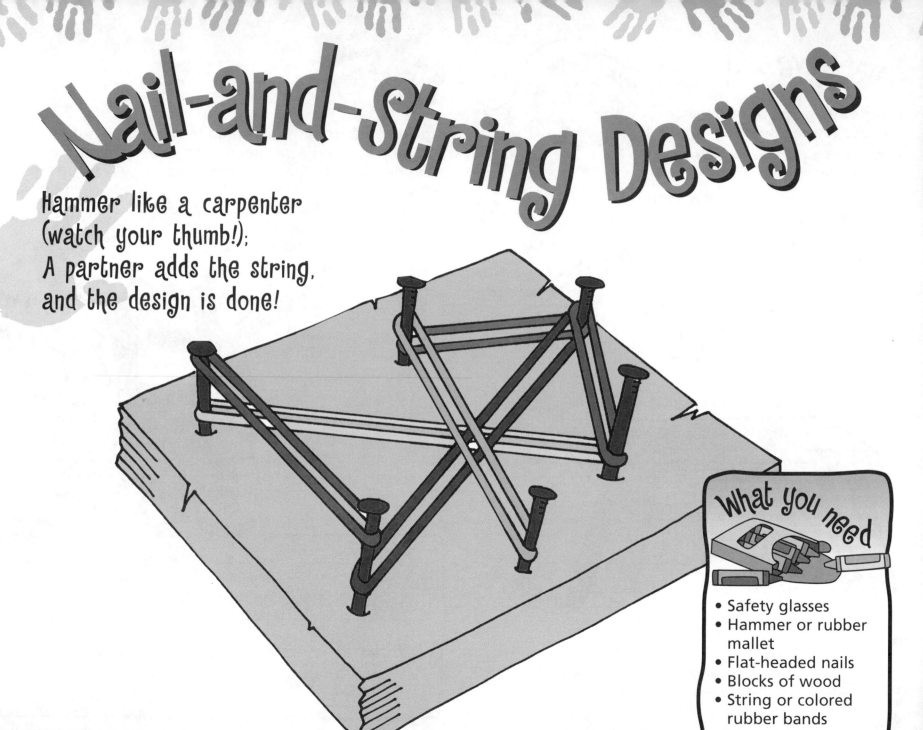

What you need

- Safety glasses
- Hammer or rubber mallet
- Flat-headed nails
- Blocks of wood
- String or colored rubber bands

Here we go!

1. Put on safety glasses. Hammer nails into separate pieces of wood.
2. Trade nailed wood pieces.
3. Make designs by wrapping string or rubber bands around the nails.

Tip: Use nails with large heads so the string or rubber bands will stay on the nails. If desired, paint the head of the nails to enhance the design.

Note: Even small children are capable of working with nails and hammers, and they get a wonderful "big kid" boost of self-esteem from doing so. However, grown-up supervision is a must. Have only two children work together at a time.

PlayTime!

Build a Boat: Nail blocks of wood of different sizes together to make a boat. Paint the top in bright colors. Glue on a wooden dowel mast and a sail!

Helping Hands

This activity is especially good for developing eye-hand coordination, exploring cause-and-effect relationships, and developing a respect for another's sense of design ... as well as celebrating what kids can make using "real" tools!

Mystery Rubbings

Something is hidden
from your eyes;
Abracadabra ...
watch the surprise!

What you need

- Masking tape
- Coins, buttons, Popsicle sticks, and other small, thin objects
- White paper
- Crayons, with paper covers removed

Here we go!

1. Tape objects onto the table without letting your partner see what you're taping.
2. Cover the objects with the white paper, taping the corners so the paper stays in place.
3. Have your partner rub crayons sideways over the paper. What objects can you "see" with the rubbings?
4. Switch roles, and make a second mystery rubbing.

PlayTime!

What's Missing? Fill a box with three to five different small objects, and show it to a partner. Now, have your partner turn around while you remove one object from the box. Ask your partner to guess what is missing. Give some hints, such as, "It was next to the red button." Then, start over and you do the guessing! (For more challenge, play with more objects.)

Story Time!

The Mystery of the Missing Red Mitten
by Steven Kellogg

Helping Hands

Invite kids to use their sense of touch to predict what objects may be under the paper before they begin the rubbings. Encourage observation about the different designs made. How do bumpy surfaces show up compared with smooth surfaces?

Shadow Tracing

"You trace me and I'll trace you."
Your shadow, my shadow;
together, we have two!

What you need

- Butcher paper
- Flashlight, lamp, or sunny window
- Crayons and markers
- Child safety scissors
- Collage materials (buttons, fabric scraps, torn paper)
- Glue

Here we go!

1. Spread the butcher paper on the floor. Stand so that you cast a shadow on the paper. Ask your partner to trace your shadow. Remember to stand very still!

2. Switch roles, so that now your partner casts the shadow and you trace.

3. Cut out the shadows.

4. Decorate them together, using markers, crayons, and collage materials.

Story Time!

Bear Shadow by Frank Asch
Shadows and Reflections by Tana Hoban
Footprints and Shadows by Anne Dodd

PlayTime!

Me and My Shadow: Trace your shadow outside at different times of day. Stand with your back toward the sun in the morning, and ask a partner to trace the outline of your feet and your body's shadow. Then, stand in the same spot at noon, and again late in the day, and have the partner trace those shadows. When does your shadow look smallest? Longest?

Flashlight Fun: Sit close to a light-colored wall. Have a partner shine a flashlight on it. Make finger shadow figures on the wall by moving your hands together in different ways in the light to create a rabbit, a butterfly, or another figure. See if your partner can guess what shadow figure you're making. Then, switch roles.

Helping Hands

Tracing shadows is fun, but it's tricky, too! The resulting shapes may not look at all like body shapes. Encourage creativity!

Rather than direct the activity, allow children to experiment together, determining on their own the best ways to stand and shine the light to make shadows.

Blow It!

Windy days
make fluttering trees.
Air through a straw
makes painting a breeze!

What you need

- Paper
- Tempera paint, watered down slightly, in a lid or dish
- Plastic drinking straws

Here we go!

1. Share a sheet of paper with a partner.
2. Take turns putting a few drops of paint onto the paper.
3. Blow through the straws to move the paint around the paper (be careful not to suck in!).

PlayTime!

Balloon Bounce: See how long you and a partner can keep a blown-up balloon from touching the ground by tapping it lightly back and forth. You'll need to work together, pushing it through the air to each other. Count each time you tap. How high did you count?

Imagine This: Pretend you are the wind. Move your body as if you are a warm summer breeze. Then, move as if you are a howling windstorm. Whoosh!

Story Time!

Feel the Wind by Arthur Dorros
Who Took the Farmer's Hat? by Joan L. Nodset
Hot-Air Henry by Mary Calhoun

Helping Hands

Encourage children to experiment with different blowing techniques: blowing together at the same time and at different times; using coffee stirrers and "crazy" straws. Ask children to predict how the paint will work and then have them test their hunches.

Mitten Match

Woolly mittens
so soft to wear;
Two paper mittens
make a pair!

What you need

- Paper, cut in the shape of mittens
- Markers and crayons
- Collage materials (fabric scraps, sequins, stickers, buttons, colored paper scraps, tissue-paper scraps)
- Glue

Here we go!

1. Decorate one mitten shape.
2. Trade decorated mittens with a partner.
3. Decorate another mitten to match the one your partner gave you. Hey, you've got a pair!

Story Time! *Runaway Mitten* by Jean Rogers
The Mitten by Jan Brett

PlayTime!

Mitten Memory Game:
Cut out 10 pairs of paper mittens and color them with different designs, leaving the backs plain. Turn the mittens facedown on a flat surface. Play a game of memory with a partner, turning up two mittens at a time. If they match, keep the pair. If they don't, turn them back over, and let your partner have a turn. Continue until all the mittens are used up; then, count your matches.

Helping Hands

By making the matches and copying patterns, children hone their observation skills and increase their awareness of how things around them are similar and different. Such experiences are crucial steps in developing logical thinking.

Sand Sculptures

Sand in a sandbox,
sand by the sea,
Sand in a pattern
made by you and me!

What you need

- Small funnel
- Small jars, with corks or lids
- Colored sand, salt, or rice
- Spoons

Here we go!

1. Place the funnel in the opening of a small jar.

2. Working with a partner, take turns spooning different colors of the sand, salt, or rice into the funnel. Tap the jar gently to level each layer.

3. Secure the filled jar with a cork or lid. What a beautiful sand scene you made together!

Tips: • Empty plastic honey bears make wonderful sand art containers.

• To make colored sand, rub a piece of colored chalk over a thin layer of sand in a small Styrofoam tray. You can also do this with clean, sifted salt or rice.

• If a wavy design is desired, poke the layers with a toothpick to mix them slightly.

PlayTime!

Sand Art Pictures: With a partner, make a sand art picture with colored sand and white glue: Place a piece of construction paper on a cookie sheet, and take turns making a design with the glue. Sprinkle different colors of sand over the glue. Let dry; then, gently turn the paper over to let the extra sand fall off.

 **Story Time!** *The Beach Day* by Douglas Florian
A Day at the Beach by Mircea Vasiliu

Helping Hands

For those times when a child doesn't want to participate in an activity with another, quickly pair the "extra" person with another partner, so that she doesn't feel embarrassed. Encourage the nonparticipant to tell you *how* she feels and *why*. Then, allow the "loner" to work alone or with a grown-up, but not to wander or pair up with a different child.

Magnet Masterpiece

Clips above, a magnet below,
paint and paper in between.
You can make a masterpiece,
by working as a team!

- Paper
- Metal cookie sheet or pie tin
- Tape
- Tempera paints, watered down slightly, various colors
- Small metal objects (paper clips, small nonsharp screws and bolts)
- Strong magnets

Here we go!

1. Place the paper on top of the cookie sheet or pie tin. Tape to hold it in place.
2. Take turns dropping small amounts of the paint onto the paper.
3. Place a few small metal objects onto the paper.
4. Hold the cookie sheet together. Take turns rubbing the magnet along the bottom of the cookie sheet.
5. Continue "painting" with magnets until you've made a design you like.

   Who are the artists — you or your magnets?

PlayTime!

Buddy-Up Ball Painting: Place a sheet of paper in a large, shallow box. Place blobs of different paint colors on the paper. Add marbles or golf balls. With a partner, move the box to create a design.

Yarn Pull: Place paper on newspaper on a flat surface. Drop blobs of paint onto paper; then, with a partner, pull a long piece of yarn across the paper to make a design. You'll have to give and take to make it work!

Story Time!

Mystery of Magnets by Melvin Berger
Red, Blue and Yellow by Miriam Kosman

We're Taking a Trip!

We've got our tickets
so don't be slow,
Help pack a bag
and away we'll go!

SUN TAM

What you need

- Poster board, cut into suitcase shapes
- Child safety scissors
- Old magazines
- Glue

Here we go!

1. With a partner, decide where you would go on a pretend trip. It can be to the beach, the mountains, to outer space — anywhere you'd both like to go.

2. Decide together what you need to take on your trip, including things you need and things you'd like to have along. Cut out pictures of those items from old magazines and glue them onto the suitcase.

3. Take a pretend trip, taking turns sharing the suitcase. How will you get to where you are going?

Tip: Make sure the suitcase pattern has a usable handle on it.

PlayTime!

What's Next? Getting ready for a trip involves a lot of steps, and it's important that they are done in the right order (you wouldn't want to get on a plane before your suitcase was packed, would you?). With a partner, cut out a series of pictures that show the steps of getting ready for a trip, taking the trip, and coming back home.

Take a Safari: Sit in a circle with others. Play the knee-thumping, hand-clapping game of taking a pretend bear or lion hunt. Take turns being the "scout" and leading others with hand motions and sounds through the tall grass, over a bridge, through the mud, and wherever else your safari takes you.

 Story Time!
"The Wheels on the Bus" (song)
Going on a Bear Hunt by Michael Rosen
Little Brown Bear Goes on a Trip by Claude Lebrun

Helping Hands

This is an excellent activity to practice cooperation and compromising skills, as well as organizational skills. For at-home fun, children can paint or decorate a cardboard cereal box and add a rope handle to make a suitcase. Fill it with the proper clothing, supplies, and treasured items needed on a real trip.

Playing All Together

(Cooperative Play in a Group)

It's lots of fun to play alone, or with just one other person. But sometimes having more kids share in the play multiples the fun, adding to the giggles. Why, with a whole group of kids, you can make a long, long circus train — or even throw a party!

Discover how much fun you can have by playing all together.

Party Time!

What you need

- Cupcake mix
- Construction paper
- Crayons
- Stapler
- Yarn or ribbon
- Frosting and edible cupcake decorations

Cake and ice cream,
games to play;
Gather together
for a special day!

Here we go!

1. Make cupcakes with a grown-up before the party. Leave unfrosted.

2. Decide on a theme for the party together. Do you want to dress up in special clothes or silly outfits, or just "come as you are"?

3. For party hats, decorate a piece of construction paper. Ask a grown-up to staple the edges together in a cone shape to fit your head. Add yarn or ribbons for ties.

4. Draw a big picture of your party theme on construction paper for a game of Pin-the-Tail-on-the-[you decide!].

5. Frost and decorate the cupcakes with sprinkles, chocolate chips, raisins — your choice. Then, in the best party tradition, eat them up!

Throw an <u>unbirthday</u> party any old time to celebrate just being together!

Story Time!

Hedgehog Bakes a Cake by Maryann MacDonald
Cook-a-Doodle-Doo! by Janet Stevens and Susan Stevens Crummel

Helping Hands

An unbirthday party presents an opportunity to talk casually about "alike" and "different" ("How is this party different from a birthday party?"). It also offers a chance to discuss "left out" feelings. Ask kids to brainstorm ways to avoid causing "left out" feelings and what to do if you have those feelings.

Fish in the Sea

1. Make paper fish out of colored construction paper. Decorate with markers and crayons.

2. Ask a grown-up to attach a paper clip* to each fish. Place fish in a large cardboard-box "sea."

3. Have a grown-up make several fishing poles (sticks or yardsticks with string tied on and a magnet* tied at the bottom of the line).

4. Take turns fishing with the poles, until you've caught all the fish in the sea.

*Note: Paper clips and small magnets pose a choking hazard to young children. Grown-ups should attach them to the project and supervise the play.

Ball in the Air

1. Form a circle around an old sheet or parachute.

2. Place lightweight balls or pom-poms onto the center of the sheet.

3. Raise the edges of the sheet and work together to bounce the balls around. Keep them on the sheet. Can you make the balls bounce around the circle slowly and then faster and faster?

Colorful Caterpillar

Fuzzy caterpillars
are fun to hold.
Together make one
big and bold!

What you need

- Small paper plates
- Tempera paints, various colors, in lids or dishes
- Paintbrushes
- Glue
- Pipe cleaners

Here we go!

1. Paint stripes, dots, squiggles — whatever you like — on your paper plate.

2. Glue your paper plate to another kid's plate. Press down and let dry. Add everyone else's plates, making a very long caterpillar.

3. Glue pipe-cleaner legs underneath the caterpillar. Decide together if your caterpillar will have lots of legs or just a few. Add pipe-cleaner "feelers," too!

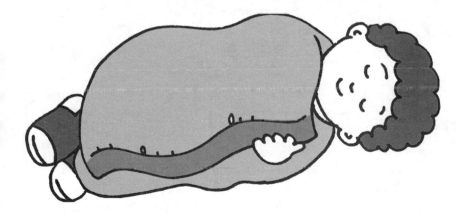

Story Time!
The Very Hungry Caterpillar by Eric Carle
The Butterfly Hunt by Yoshi
Where Butterflies Grow by Joanne Ryder

PlayTime!

Caterpillar Collage: Decorate your caterpillar by gluing fabric, beads, tissue paper, and other craft materials onto the plates.

Nature Hunt: Go on a nature walk with a grown-up and look for caterpillars in gardens, on leaves, or on the ground. Look at the book *Monarch Magic!* by Lynn M. Rosenblatt to see beautiful pictures of a caterpillar changing into a butterfly.

Make-Believe Fun: Crawl around the room like a caterpillar, and pretend to eat leaves. Make yourself a cocoon with blankets. When you come out as a beautiful butterfly, dry your wings and gently fly away!

Helping Hands

By encouraging each child to decorate his plate as he wishes, you reinforce the idea that you can express your individuality while still cooperating in a group effort.

Circus Train

With a group of kids creating together, you can make this train the longest ever!

What you need

- Long sheet of paper
- Kitchen sponges
- Tempera paint, various colors and black, in separate trays
- Empty thread spools
- Black yarn
- Glue
- Child safety scissors
- Stickers or animals from old magazines

Here we go!

1. Lay out the paper on a long, flat table or the floor.

2. Take turns dipping sponges in the paint. Sponge-paint train-car rectangles onto the paper.

3. Make train wheels by dipping the end of the thread spool into the black paint, and printing under the train cars. Let paint dry.

4. Glue pictures of animals cut from magazines onto the train car (or use stickers). Glue black yarn over the animals to create cages, and connect the cars with yarn "couplings."

PlayTime!

Train Ride: Line up chairs two by two. Invite some kids to go on a ride. Take turns being the conductor. Describe what you see and let your passengers guess where you are going.

Travel Talk: What's your favorite way to travel? By car, plane, bus, boat, or train? Share a story about a trip you've taken and how you got there.

Play Train, Truck, Track: Sit in a circle and make up a silly story with *T* words. Each person adds a line to the story, using words that sound like the beginning of the word *train*. "I took a *truck* to the *track*." "I went on a *train* to the store to buy a *tricycle*." Don't worry if the story doesn't make sense — it's just for fun! Terrific!

 Story Time!

Freight Train by Donald Crews
The Little Engine That Could by Watty Piper

Helping Hands

As children tell stories about travel, ask questions that encourage the use of descriptive words, so they "paint a picture" with their words.

Milk-Jug Catch

First it's a milk jug, now it's a toy
for catching a ball tossed by a girl or boy.
Gather a group of kids today,
all together, keep the balls in play!

What you need

- Plastic milk jugs, 1-gallon (4-L) size
- Sharp scissors (for grown-up use only)
- Stickers, fabric, paper, glitter, permanent markers, and other decorations
- Glue
- Balls of different sizes (tennis balls, table-tennis balls, wiffle balls)

Here we go!

1. Ask a grown-up to cut a section out of the milk jugs, as shown.

2. Decorate the jugs with assorted decorations and markers.

3. When your jug is decorated and the glue has dried, play a game of catch, using the decorated jugs as "mitts." For more fun, try using balls of different sizes.

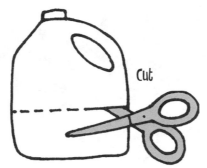

Cut

Decorate

GLUE

Story Time! *Stop That Ball!* by Mike McClintock
Catch the Ball! by Eric Carle

PlayTime!

Ball Line-Up: Order balls by weight or size, from lightest to heaviest or smallest to largest. Toss them, one at a time, to a partner. Now switch, so that you're the catcher. Did you toss and catch the different balls in different ways?

Rainy-Day Fun: Play catch indoors by rolling the balls on the floor from one jug to another.

Helping Hands

Encourage kids to play as one team, working together rather than competing, so that each person in the group feels equally valued. Recognize cooperative behavior: "I see Rebecca, Dylanie, and James are working together to keep the ball in play."

Bowling Bottles

Colorful pins
set up tall.
Knock them down
and watch them fall!

What you need

- Tissue paper, various colors
- Glue, slightly watered down
- Plastic bottles from water or soda, with lids, 6 total
- Rubber ball, for bowling

Here we go!

1. Rip tissue paper into small pieces.
2. Apply glue to the outsides of the bottles.
3. Cover the glue with tissue paper. Let dry.
4. Gather six decorated bottles together and set them up in bowling-pin formation as shown.
5. Take turns knocking the pins down by rolling a rubber ball and then setting the pins back up again for the next player.

PlayTime!

Sports Survey: Bowling is just one of many games you can play as a team. What are some of your other favorite group games? Duck, Duck, Goose or Tag? Ask everyone to name one favorite. How will you decide together on one game to play?

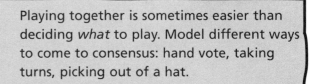

Helping Hands

Playing together is sometimes easier than deciding *what* to play. Model different ways to come to consensus: hand vote, taking turns, picking out of a hat.

House of Friends

Our little house
is oh so sweet.
We all take turns
to keep it neat.

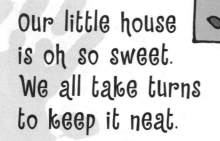

What you need

- Refrigerator or other large appliance box
- Sharp scissors or utility knife (for grown-up use only)
- Paintbrushes
- Tempera paints, various colors
- Glue
- Decorations
- Paper and markers

Here we go!

1. With two or three kids, decide how you'd like your house to look. Talk about where you'd like windows, a door, maybe even some shutters.
2. Ask a grown-up to cut out the openings.
3. Together, paint the sides, windows, and door.
4. Glue on other decorations to make your house special.
5. Make a sign with your names to hang on the door, such as "Alexa, Lisa, Eric, and Jacob's House." Don't forget to add a doormat that says "Welcome!"

Plan what it would be like to live with a few other children (and no grown-ups!). Who will cook? Who will clean? If everyone works together, you can turn your house into a home!

PlayTime!

A Home Is: Is your home in a house or an apartment? Is it in the country or in the city? Homes can be as different as an igloo made of snow and a tepee made of animal skins. The most important things in a home, of course, are the people! Tell what you like best about your home.

Nature Fun: Look for animal homes with a grown-up. Don't forget to look up in the trees or under bushes and leaves. How many different animal homes can you find?

Story Time!

How a House Is Built by Gail Gibbons
A House Is a House for Me by Mary Ann Hoberman
A House for Hermit Crab by Eric Carle

Helping Hands

This activity is a real challenge for kids (and adults, too!). If a natural leader evolves in a group, guide her to help organize —rather than making all the decisions herself and becoming "the boss." Model noncontrolling behavior: "Who would like to paint the back door?" not "You have to paint the back door brown."

Cooperative Calendar

Cross off the days
one by one;
With a group
it's lots of fun!

What you need

- White paper
- Markers
- Crayons
- Large construction paper or poster board, 12 pieces
- Glue
- Copies of a monthly calendar

Here we go!

1. Have a grown-up draw lines to divide each piece of paper into four equal sections, and write the name of one of the 12 months at the top of each paper.

2. Use markers and crayons to make a picture in one of the sections on each sheet.

3. Pass the paper to someone else, and have her add another picture for that month. Continue trading pictures until each piece of paper is filled with four drawings by different kids. (The final drawing for April, for instance, will have four April pictures from four different children.)

4. On the construction paper or poster board, attach the printed days of the months under the appropriate pictures. Place the months in order. Hang up your calendar and mark off the days in different colors.

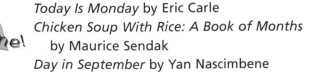

Today Is Monday by Eric Carle
Chicken Soup With Rice: A Book of Months by Maurice Sendak
Day in September by Yan Nascimbene

PlayTime!

Weather Watch: Each day one person gets to draw a symbol for that day's weather — a sun, clouds, snowflakes, raindrops — on the calendar date.

It's a Tradition: What special traditions do you or other kids celebrate? List them all on your calendar.

Helping Hands

A good way to help children learn time and sequence patterns (like days and months) is to attach significance to them. Point out patterns repeatedly: "On Tuesdays, we always go to the library; on Fridays, we always have a special snack."

Paper Pizza

Ruby   Jared

Sally   Carlos   Jessie

Pizza, pizza, pizza pie
cheese on top, my oh my!
Cut in slices, five or more,
piled high with foods galore!

What you need

- Child safety scissors
- Red and yellow (or white) construction paper
- Glue stick
- Old magazines

Here we go!

1. Cut the yellow or white paper into the shape of a large, round pizza. Cut a smaller circle out of the red paper (to be the sauce), and glue it onto the other circle.

2. Cut out pictures of foods that the group likes.

3. Glue the pictures onto the pizza. Will everyone's favorite foods be mixed together or will the pizza circle be divided into slices?

4. Write the name of each pizza cook along the outside edge.

PlayTime!

Pizza Party: Make a real pizza with a grown-up and others. Yum!

Story Time!

Green Eggs and Ham by Dr. Seuss
Bread and Jam for Frances by Russell Hoban
Gregory, the Terrible Eater by Mitchell Sharmat

Rainbow Prints

Beautiful rainbow
in the sky —
Colors together
way up high.

What you need

- Paintbrush
- Tempera paints,
  the colors of the
  rainbow: red,
  orange, yellow,
  green, blue,
  indigo, violet
- Large sheet of
  butcher paper

Here we go!

1. Paint your hands red, and make handprints in one corner of the paper. Wash your hands.

2. Have another kid make orange handprints next to your red ones, in a curved row. (Wash hands after each color.)

3. Continue taking turns, with one or several kids, making handprints in curved rows of color: yellow, then green, then blue, indigo (bright blue), and violet (purple-blue). Wow! What a beautiful rainbow, made by different hands working together!

PlayTime!

Category Call: With other kids, form a circle, holding onto an old sheet or a parachute. A grown-up calls out a color cue ("All kids with yellow shirts to the middle!"), and all kids who fit that color cue run into the center, under the sheet. Keep playing until everyone has been included.

Story Time!

All the Colors We Are: The Story of How We Get Our Skin Color by Katie Kissinger
The Rainbow Fish by Marcus Pfister
Rainbow Joe and Me by Maria Diaz Strom

Helping Hands

Using a simple cooperative activity, such as these colorful handprints, can help kids develop a respect for differences. Point out that all the handprints, with their different colors, contribute *equally* to the overall rainbow.

Name Art

A, B, C —
the letters go.
Which one starts
the name you know?

What you need

- Crayons, markers, colored pencils
- Paper

Here we go!

1. Write the first letter of your name in large print on a piece of paper.
2. Trade letter papers with a partner.
3. Make a picture using the first letter of your partner's name.

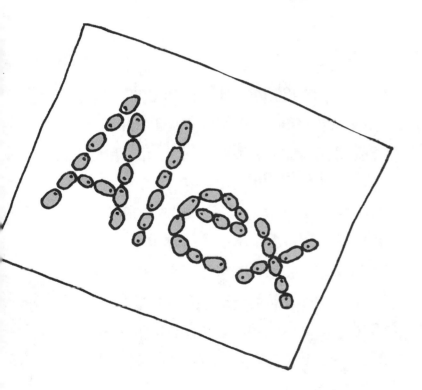

PlayTime!

Phonics Fun: Cut out pictures from old magazines of things that begin with the same letter sound as your partner's name, and glue them to the paper.

Bean Art: Write all the letters of your first name in large print on a piece of paper. Trade name papers with a partner. Glue beans onto your partner's name.

What's the Story? Ask a grown-up about your name. Were you named after someone in your family, or was your name one that your parents especially liked? Compare name stories with a partner.

Story Time!

A My Name Is Alice by Jane Bayer
ABC by Anne Geddes
Dr. Seuss's ABC

Helping Hands

By exploring names, you'll help children appreciate their special identity. Names that are the same can be a springboard for discussing last names and middle names, reinforcing that all people are different.

PLAYING ALL TOGETHER 81

Can We Talk About It?

(Communication Play)

Communication is letting other people know how we feel and what we think. We greet someone with a big "Hi!" and talk on the phone. But talking is only part of it. We communicate with our bodies, too, without saying a word! Winks, waves, frowns, and funny faces are all ways to communicate — and so are songs and giggles! And don't forget all the messages you send in cards, notes, and even on a computer!

Body Talk

Head down,
big frown.
Head high,
smiling eyes!

The expression on your face; the way you hold your head, arms, and hands; and even the way you stand can tell a lot to another person — even if you don't say a word! In fact, your body is "talking" all the time. Body language tells others how we are feeling about ourselves and about them.

Here we go!

1. Use your body to communicate some of these ideas, and ask your partner to guess what you are saying:

   "Hi!"

   "Bye!"

   "Be quiet, please"

   "Come here, please"

   "I'm angry!"

   "I'm feeling shy"

   "Stop!"

   "Yuck!"

   "Yummmm!"

   "Wow!"

2. Switch roles, so that you're doing the guessing and your partner is "body talking."

Helping Hands

Watch for body language, because kids feeling poorly — physically or emotionally — often communicate most openly with facial expressions and stance. Monitor their conflicting feelings by being aware of the contradictory messages you get from their words and their body language.

Say What?

Body language can be confusing. Suppose your mom says, "Everything's fine," but you can tell she isn't. What should you do? Say what you notice, and then offer to help out. "I know you <u>said</u> you are fine, Mom, but you don't <u>seem</u> fine. I'll help you set the table tonight, OK?" Way to go — you're great!

PlayTime!

What Am I? Use your eyes to listen! One person acts out an animal's movements — a swinging monkey, a lumbering elephant, a hopping bunny — in front of the rest of the group without talking. The first person to guess the correct animal becomes the next actor. Play until each kid has had a turn at being the animal.

Learn American Sign Language! American Sign Language (ASL) is a way hearing-impaired people can communicate, without needing to speak. There are hand signs for each letter of the alphabet and also for expressions and phrases that are used frequently.

Story Time!

Happy Birthday!: A Beginner's Book of Signs by Angela Bednarczyk and Janet Weinstock
The Handmade Alphabet and *The Handmade Counting Book* by Laura Rankin

Phone Fun

Ring, ring, ring,
it's a call for you!
Talk with a pal
for a moment or two.

What you need

• Cardboard tubes, 2
• Markers and crayons
• Yarn

Here we go!

1. With a partner, decorate the cardboard tubes. With help, make a small hole near the bottom of each tube.
2. Thread the yarn through each hole; tie a knot in the end.
3. Holding the line tight, talk and listen to your partner through your phony phones.

PlayTime!

Long Distance: With a grown-up's help, call up a friend or relative who lives far away and talk on the phone. Listen carefully, and speak clearly into the receiver. Aren't you happy that you called?

Calling 911! Are you learning to use the phone at home? Ask a grown-up to write the numbers you should call in an emergency in big numerals next to the phone. That way you can "dial" them yourself if you need help! Make a pretend telephone keypad to practice.

 **Story Time!** *Mice Squeak, We Speak* by Tomie dePaola

Thanks to Sarah Williamson for her help with this activity, adapted from *Fun With My 5 Senses*.

Helping Hands

Take turns with the phony phone modeling good phone etiquette. Show kids how to identify themselves and how to ask to speak to a friend; how to take a message and how to leave a message. Together, make a message pad to keep by the telephone at home. Discuss what an "emergency" means. "Is a spilled glass of milk an emergency? What about a lost toy?"

Lend an Ear

A quiet time
with listening ears,
Shows a pal
that someone hears.

Here we go!

1. Spend some together time with someone who seems sad.

2. Invite that pal to play a board game or play with a toy that you can share together — just the two of you.

3. Ask the person what he has been thinking about or doing. Then, sit quietly and listen to what he has to say.

4. If the person doesn't want to talk, play quietly together. Just being together is a very important way to say, "I like you, and I'm sorry you're sad!"

Safe Speaking Zone

Sometimes you might feel like talking, and other times you might not want to talk at all. That's just fine. The important thing to know is that if you have something on your mind, you can tell someone you trust. Think about the people you can talk to if something is bothering you.

Thanks to Sarah Williamson for her help with this activity, adapted from *Fun With My 5 Senses*.

PlayTime!

I feel sad when...

Sad-to-Glad Art: Using a pencil, you and a partner each draw pictures of a sad face with tears. With grown-up help, write down something that might make you sad on the bottom of your picture. Now, switch pictures. Talk about how you can make each other feel better, and have a grown-up write your ideas on the papers ("I would give Alexa a hug." "I would share my special dog with Justin"). Then, erase the tears on your partner's picture, add a smile, and hand it back!

 **Story Time!**

Abuela by Arthur Dorros
Let's Talk About: Feeling Sad by Joy Berry
Why So Sad, Brown Rabbit? by Sheridan Cain

 **Helping Hands**

Being a good, attentive listener is one way to help cheer up a child who is feeling sad. Ask her, in a quiet place, what is bothering her. Let her talk; then, repeat what she says so she knows she's been heard. Support her feelings. Then ask her to be your special helper for a little while. It's amazing how children respond to positive one-on-one attention.

Traffic Signs

Red light, green light,
yellow light, too;
Signs and symbols
help me and you!

What you need

- Poster board
- Crayons or markers
- Glue or staples
- Cardboard paper-
  towel tubes

Here we go!

1. Make traffic and information signs.
2. Glue or staple your signs onto paper-towel tubes so that they are easy to hold up.
3. Play a traffic game. Choose some people to be the sign holders, and the rest to be the cars and trucks. The sign holders stand in different spots around the room, and the traffic moves around them. Then, switch roles. Are there any signs you need to add to make the traffic move more smoothly?

PlayTime!

On the Go! The next time you ride in a car or on a bus, notice the shapes and colors of the signs you see. What do you do when you see an eight-sided sign that's red?

Play Red Light, Green Light: One person (the leader) stands about five kid-lengths apart from the others, her back to the group. When she says, "Green light," everyone else starts walking toward her. When she says, "Red light," she turns around and everyone stops walking. Anyone the leader catches still moving must go back to the start. Continue until someone tags the leader, and becomes the new "traffic light."

Make Your Own: Using plain paper plates, markers, construction paper, and glue, make a sign that instantly tells a message in a picture. Try an "I'm sad" sign, a "Keep out!" or a "Come in!" sign.

Story Time! *I See a Sign* by Lars Klove
I Read Signs by Tana Hoban

In Print

Thankyou for helping me.

Make a picture,
sign it, too,
Then send a message —
from me to you!

Here we go!

1. Make a card or note for someone. Use bright colors, or cut the paper in an interesting shape.
2. Draw a happy picture and write a nice thought in words: "Thank you for helping me." "I like your new red shirt." "You are fun!" — whatever special message you feel like sending.
3. Sign your name.
4. Leave your message where your special someone will be sure to see it.

PlayTime!

Post Office: With a group of kids or your family, decorate shoe boxes. Put one kid's name on each box. Ask a grown-up to make a mail slot in each lid. Place your homemade mailboxes in a row on a windowsill or on a table. Send pictures or notes back and forth.

Mail a Message: Send a picture you've drawn or a letter to a special friend or relative by mail. Ask a grown-up to write  down, or help you write, what you want to say. Then, go to the post office to mail it together. (Don't forget the stamp!) You might even get a letter back!

Computer Fun: With a grown-up, send an e-mail message to someone you know. Ask for help typing and transmitting.

 Story Time!

The Jolly Postman: or Other People's Letters by Janet and Allan Ahlberg
A Letter to Amy by Ezra Jack Keats
Love, Your Bear Pete by Dylan Sheldon

Please—and Thank You!

Words to share
That show
you care!

What you need

- Child safety scissors
- Old magazines with photos of people
- Empty half-pint milk carton (250 ml)
- Glue

Here we go!

1. With a partner, cut out six pictures from magazines of people of different ages in different situations — a kid eating ice cream, an older person with a cane, kids waving to each other, a parent reading to a child, and so on.

2. Make a large die from the empty milk carton, flattening down the top.

3. Glue a picture on each side of the die.

4. To play, roll the milk-carton die. Then, say a helpful phrase that fits the picture rolled, as if you were part of the scene. Take turns until you've "rolled" all the pictures.

Flatten top

Glue pictures

Story Time! *Manners* by Aliki

Encourage respectful behavior by modeling and acknowledging caring words and actions. Children are quick to model behavior that elicits a positive response. Try acting out different situations, switching grown-up and kid roles so that kids are modeling the appropriate phrases and behaviors, "teaching" the grown-up.

Helping Hands

Sing Out

Sing high,
sing low.
Sing out all the songs
you know!

What you need

- White paper
- Crayons and markers
- Construction paper
- Stapler

Here we go!

1. Ask a grown-up to write the words to your favorite songs on white paper, one song per page. Include songs for every child.

2. Draw pictures on the papers to illustrate the songs.

3. Put all decorated pages together in a book with construction-paper covers. Staple.

4. Title the songbook *Our Favorite Songs*. Decorate the cover. Now, sing!

PlayTime!

Create a Band: With others, decorate different-sized containers to make homemade instruments. Fill them with objects that make different sounds — the louder, the better! Then, play together in your own marching band!

Clapping Clues: Play this game with two or more kids. Hide an object; then, as the searcher looks for it, use louder clapping to indicate "You're close" or soft clapping to say, "You're far away." Play until the object is found, and then play again until everyone has had a turn being the searcher.

My Five Senses by Aliki
Margret & H. A. Rey's Curious George at the Parade
Too Much Noise by Ann McGovern

A Rainbow of Feelings

(Exploring Emotions)

Silly, happy, mad, or lonely — from morning to night, many different emotions color our days. What should we do with all those feelings? Express them! Discover how to "let out" your big bundle of emotions in appropriate ways. And as you have fun exploring your rainbow of feelings, you'll get to know a very special person — you! — just a little bit better!

Colorful Feelings

Sad

Happy

What you need

- Paper
- Crayons and markers

Happy colors, silly colors —
wild colors, too!
What different feelings
do colors "say" to you?

Here we go!

1. Draw pictures that show what colors you'd use to express different feelings: "glad feeling" colors, "yucky feeling" colors, "awesome feeling" colors, and "sleepy, droopy feeling" colors.

2. Ask a grown-up to help you label each "color feeling" picture: "glad" colors, "mad" colors, and so on.

3. Compare your color feeling pictures with another person's. Do you "feel" colors the same way or differently?

My "GLAD" COLORS

MY "SAD" COLORS

JOE

Story Time!

My Many Colored Days by Dr. Seuss
Feelings by Aliki
Double-Dip Feelings: Stories to Help Children Understand Emotions by Barbara S. Cain

Helping Hands

Colors are a good way to introduce feelings because kids don't really have to "own" those feelings. Let kids sponge-print individual pages with vivid primary colors, some earth tones, and some neon colors. Hold each color up and ask, "Does this color make you feel happy, mad, wild, or calm?" Give choices at first to introduce kids to a broad spectrum of "feeling" words. Then, encourage kids to respond without prompting: "What's the feeling that you'd put with this color?"

PlayTime!

Color Feeling Spin: Make a spinner by coloring pie-shaped sections of a large paper plate in different colors. Cut an arrow out of construction paper; ask a grown-up to attach it to the spinner with a paper fastener*. Sit in a circle with others. The first child spins to a color, then says the feeling that color makes her think of. Pass the spinner around the circle until everyone has had a turn. Then, spin it some more!

***Note:** Paper fasteners pose choking and poking danger to small children. Adults should control the supply and insert them into the project. Be sure to put away all unused fasteners.

Our Feelings Book

Silly, shy, lonely, scared —
These are feelings we've all shared!

Silly - by Suzy

SAD - by Eric

What you need

- Camera and film
- Glue
- Construction paper
- Markers
- Hole punch
- Yarn

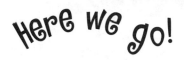

Here we go!

1. Gather a group of kids. Have a grown-up take separate photos* of each of you making faces that show you feeling different ways — angry, scared, silly, happy, surprised, jealous, disappointed, sad, relaxed, bored — you decide!

2. Glue each picture onto a different sheet of construction paper.

3. Write the word for each feeling underneath its picture, along with the "actor's" name: "Silly" by Suzanne; "Sad" by Eric.

4. Punch holes in the papers and tie them together with yarn. Write *Our Feelings Book* on the cover. Fantastic!

*Tip: If a camera isn't available, cut out faces with different feeling expressions from magazines.

What Makes Me Happy? by Catherine and Laurence Anholt
Little Feelings by Judy Spain Barton
How Are You Peeling? Foods with Moods by Saxton Freymann and Joost Elffers

PlayTime!

Emotion Sandwich: You and a partner spread cream cheese on different pieces of bread. Talk about how you're feeling; then, make a raisin face in the cream cheese to reflect those emotions. When you've finished your faces, put the slices together and make a sandwich. Then, cut it in half and share it!

Helping Hands

When kids can't put the correct name to the feeling, they often have a hard time expressing it appropriately. Encourage kids to name their feelings out loud in "I" messages: "I feel mad when Mommy goes on a business trip." Actually, "mad" may not really be the feeling at all — "lonely" or "scared" or "forgotten" may be more accurate. Acknowledge the stated feeling and then ask open-ended questions to guide kids to refine that feeling further. *Naming the feeling accurately* is the first step in expressing it and resolving the issue.

Expression Bingo

Act out emotions,
give them a name,
Then find those feelings
in this bingo game!

What you need

- Face expression photos (see page 103) or cutout expression pictures from old magazines
- Cardboard
- Tape
- Index cards, cut to size as needed

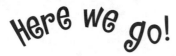

Here we go!

1. Ask a grown-up to photocopy the expression pictures in Our Feelings Book (see page 102), or cut pictures showing different emotions out of old magazines.*

2. Make "expression bingo" cards by taping the copied pictures in rows onto cardboard.

3. To play, one child acts out an emotion while the others find the photo of that same emotion on their cards and cover it up with an index card.

4. Continue playing until someone covers up one row of photos and calls out, "Expression Bingo!" Take turns acting out the emotions for each new game.

*Tip: If cutout pictures are used, make sure each card has the same *set* of emotions, even if the individual pictures are different.

Listen to My Feelings by Ruth Reardon
Happy and Sad by Alison Lester

Kids move through their days with a whole bundle of feelings — ecstatic, upset, and everything between. Provide kids with an opportunity to express their feelings when they arrive at home or school. Listen, and sincerely acknowledge their feelings without passing judgment or trying to change them.

Puppet Play

Make a puppet,
put on a play.
Let everyone know
how you feel today!

What you need

- Crayons or markers
- Paper lunch bags
- Glue
- Yarn and other
  decorations

Here we go!

1. Color paper lunch bags to make animal or people faces that represent different feelings: a brave lion, a shy mouse, a scary dragon, a sad or silly clown — any feelings you and others can think of. Glue on yarn hair or other decorations.

2. With others, make up and act out a story that includes all of the kids and puppets. One person (and puppet) starts the story ("Once upon a time there was a brave lion …"), and the next person adds a line to include a new puppet ("… that was afraid of a tiny, shy mouse. One day the shy mouse …"), and on it goes!

PlayTime!

On Stage: Make a puppet stage behind a couch or a table turned on its side. Practice your story; then, tell it to an audience. You're awesome!

 **Story Time!**

Today I Feel Silly by Jamie Lee Curtis
Faces by Anne Geddes
Silly (How I Feel) by Marcia Leonard

 **Helping Hands**

Puppetry and other dramatic play are excellent ways to "discuss" feelings without causing kids to feel exposed or vulnerable. As they "try on" feelings in character, they can explore their own emotions.

Flag That Feeling!

What makes you giggle?
What makes you sigh?
Sort different feelings
and raise them high!

What you need

- Child safety scissors
- Old magazines
- Glue stick
- Small white paper plates
- Stapler
- Paper-towel tubes

Here we go!

To make the flags:

1. Cut out pictures from magazines of people showing different emotions.

2. Sort the feeling pictures into groups: silly pictures, lonely pictures, and so on.

3. Glue each feeling group onto different paper plates, one feeling per plate.

4. Glue or staple a paper-towel tube to the bottom of each plate.

To play: Ask a grown-up to suggest a pretend situation (getting a new bike, for instance). Hold up the paper-plate flags that show how the situation would make you feel, while others hold up flags that show how that same situation would make them feel. It's fine if those feelings are different!

I Hate You! I Like You! by Tomek Bogacki
Sheila Rae, the Brave by Kevin Henkes
Love You Forever by Robert Munsch
Will You Come Back for Me? by Ann Tompert

Helping Hands

Feelings — hurt and happy — are part of every person's experience. Guide children through role-playing to acknowledge the feeling of the moment, and find an appropriate way to express it so that they can use these skills in real-life situations. Model how you might express those same feelings.

Not-So-Scary Monster Masks

A scary mask
is a frightening sight,
But beneath it is
a pal, just right!

What you need

- Scissors (for grown-up use only)
- Large paper plates, 2
- Markers, crayons, or paints
- Collage materials
- Glue
- Tongue depressors or craft sticks

Here we go!

1. Ask a grown-up to cut eye holes in the paper plates.

2. You and a partner each decorate paper plates to look like scary monsters. Let masks dry. Glue a tongue depressor beneath each mask, sticking down.

3. Trade masks. Hold the masks in front of your faces and act like monsters together.

4. Remove your masks. Underneath, there is your partner, who's not scary at all!

PlayTime!

Closet Monsters: On a piece of construction paper, draw things that scare you. On the back of the paper, draw pictures of things that comfort you. Sandwich the pictures between two sheets of construction paper. Staple one edge of the papers. Open the paper door to see what scares you, and then open the "comforting" closet.

Story Time!

Where the Wild Things Are by Maurice Sendak
Milk and Cookies by Frank Asch
Little Polar Bear and the Brave Little Hare
   by Hans de Beer
Who's Afraid of the Dark? by Crosby Bonsall

Helping Hands

Many children are afraid of monsters, the dark, and all sorts of imaginary things. Rather than dismiss these very real fears, help children see beyond them. Get kids talking about their fears and what they can do to manage those fears (look under the bed, sleep with the light on, look at the twinkling stars, tell a trusted grown-up).

Angry Confetti

Sally gets angry when she feels left out.

Juan gets angry when he gets hurt.

Sean feels angry when he gets teased.

Angry, mad —
feeling bad;
say it out loud
to lift that cloud.

What you need

- Construction paper, several colors
- Glue
- White poster board
- Pen or markers

Here we go!

1. Take turns with another kid telling each other what makes you angry, using "I" statements: "I feel angry when my braids get pulled." Each time you mention something, tear off a piece of colorful construction paper. You use one color for your "angries," and your partner uses another.

2. When you are done talking and ripping, work together to glue all the pieces onto one big sheet of white poster board.

3. With a grown-up's help, write down some of the things that make you or your partner angry ("Lisa gets angry if she's teased." "Janean gets angry if people whisper around her.").

4. Hang up your "angry" board together!

PlayTime!

Angry Clay Play: Try letting your anger or frustration out by squeezing or pounding on clay. Then, shape the clay into something that makes you happy.

Helping Hands

This activity identifies cause and effect of a feeling and can help kids realize that they "own" their feelings. The next step is to realize they can change those feelings!

When children are involved in a conflict, listen carefully to what each of them has to say. Help them see how they share the problem, and encourage them to come up with their own solutions. Then, help them put their plan into action.

Story Time!

When I Feel Angry by Cornelia Maude Spelman
Let's Talk About: Feeling Angry by Joy Berry
Andrew's Angry Words by Dorothea Lachner
Alexander and the Terrible, Horrible, No Good, Very Bad Day by Judith Viorst

Take a Break!

Here we go!

1. Spend some quiet time all by yourself, thinking about what is really bothering you and also about things that make you feel good.

2. Look at a favorite book, color a picture with crayons, or cuddle up with a favorite stuffed animal to sort out your feelings and to lift your spirits.

3. Enjoy your special time alone. Don't rush back into the group until you're ready.

Do you ever have a day when things don't seem to go your way? Take a break from being together, and join back in when you feel better!

Thanks to Sarah Williamson for help with this activity, adapted from *Fun With My 5 Senses*.

Resources for Parents and Teachers

Creative Conflict Resolution: More Than 200 Activities for Keeping Peace in the Classroom (K–6) by William J. Kreidler. Addison Wesley Longman, Inc., 1990.

Energize! Energizers and Other Great Cooperative Activities for All Ages by Carol Apacki. Quest International, Inc., 1991.

Growing Good Kids: 28 Activities to Enhance Self-Awareness, Compassion, and Leadership by Deb Delisle and Jim Delisle. Free Spirit Publishing, Inc., 1996.

How to Talk So Kids Will Listen & Listen So Kids Will Talk by Adele Faber and Elaine Mazlish. Avon Books, 1999.

Learning the Skills of Peacemaking: An Activity Guide for Elementary-Age Children on Communicating, Cooperating, Resolving Conflict by Naomi Drew. Jalmar Press, 1990.

Linking Literature With Self-Esteem by Shirley Cook and Jan Keeling. Incentive Publications, Inc., 1991.

The Mother's Almanac (rev. ed.) by Marguerite Kelly and Elia Parsons. Doubleday, 1975.

Parenting With Respect and Peacefulness: The Most Difficult Job in the World by Louise A. Dietzel. Starburst Publishers, 1995.

Parenting Young Children: Systematic Training for Effective Parenting of Children Under Six by Don C. Dinkmeyer, et al. Random House, 1997.

The Parent's Handbook: Systematic Training for Effective Parenting by Don C. Dinkmeyer and Gary D. McKay. American Guidance Service, Inc., 1997.

Positive Discipline for Preschoolers: For Their Early Years — Raising Children Who Are Responsible, Respectful, and Resourceful by Jane Nelson, Cheryl Erwin, and Roslyn Duffy. Prima Communications, Inc., 1998.

Promoting Social and Emotional Learning: Guidelines for Educators by Maurice J. Elias. The Association for Supervision and Curriculum Development, 1997.

Raising Compassionate, Courageous Children in a Violent World by Janice Cohn. Longstreet Press, 1996.

Teaching Young Children in Violent Times: Building a Peaceable Classroom by Diane E. Levin. New Society Publishing, 1994.

Thinking, Feeling, Behaving: An Emotional Education Curriculum for Children (Grades 1–6) by Ann Vernon. Research Press, 1989.

You Can't Say You Can't Play by Vivian Gussin Paley. Harvard University Press, 1992.

Activity Index

More Good Books
from
Williamson Publishing Co.

Williamson books are available from your bookseller or directly from Williamson Publishing.
Please see the last page for ordering information or to visit our website. Thank you.

Little Hands® Books . . .
***SETTING THE STAGE
FOR LEARNING!***

- **Build early learning skills**

- **Support all learning styles**

- **Promote self-esteem**

The following *Little Hands*® books for ages 2 to 7 are each 128 to 144 pages, fully illustrated, trade paper, 10 x 8, $12.95 US.

**AROUND-THE-WORLD
ART & ACTIVITIES
Visiting the 7 Continents through Craft Fun**
by Judy Press

**ArtStarts
FOR LITTLE HANDS!
Fun & Discoveries for 3- to 7-Year-Olds**
by Judy Press

**Little Hands PAPER PLATE CRAFTS
Creative Art Fun for 3- to 7-Year-Olds**
by Laura Check

**WOW! I'M READING!
Fun Activities to Make Reading Happen**
by Jill Frankel Hauser

• Parent's Guide Children's Media Award
**ALPHABET ART
With A to Z Animal Art & Fingerplays**
by Judy Press

• Real Life Award
• Children's Book-of-the-Month Club Main Selection
**The Little Hands ART BOOK
Exploring Arts & Crafts with 2- to 6-Year-Olds**
by Judy Press

• Parents' Choice Approved
**The Little Hands
BIG FUN CRAFT BOOK
Creative Fun for 2- to 6-Year-Olds**
by Judy Press

• Early Childhood News Directors' Choice Award
• Parents' Choice Approved
• Parent's Guide Children's Media Award
**SCIENCE PLAY!
Beginning Discoveries for 2- to 6-Year-Olds**
by Jill Frankel Hauser

• American Bookseller Pick of the Lists
**RAINY DAY PLAY!
Explore, Create, Discover, Pretend**
by Nancy Fusco Castaldo

- *Parents' Choice Gold Award*
- *Children's Book-of-the-Month Club Selection*

FUN WITH MY 5 SENSES
Activities to Build Learning Readiness
by Sarah A. Williamson

- *Early Childhood News Directors' Choice Award*
- *Parents' Choice Approved*

SHAPES, SIZES & MORE SURPRISES!
A Little Hands Early Learning Book
by Mary Tomczyk

- *Parents' Choice Approved*

The Little Hands NATURE BOOK
Earth, Sky, Critters & More
by Nancy Fusco Castaldo

MATH PLAY!
80 Ways to Count & Learn
by Diane McGowan and Mark Schrooten

Kids Can!® Books . . .
WHERE ALL KIDS
CAN SOAR!

- **Encourage questioning and
  self-expression**
- **Learning experiences to grow with**
- **Kids dig them!**

The following *Kids Can!*® books for ages 5 to 13 are each 144 to 178 pages, fully illustrated, trade paper, 11 x 8 1/2, $12.95 US.

Williamson's Creative, Active Fun Books

- *American Bookseller Pick of the Lists*
- *Oppenheim Toy Portfolio Best Book Award*
- *Parents' Choice Approved*
- *Parent's Guide Children's Media Award*

SUMMER FUN!
60 Activities for a Kid-Perfect Summer
by Susan Williamson

- *Selection of Book-of-the Month;
  Scholastic Book Clubs*

KIDS COOK!
Fabulous Food for the Whole Family
by Sarah Williamson & Zachary Williamson

- *Benjamin Franklin Best Multicultural
  Book Award*
- *Parents' Choice Approved*
- *Skipping Stones Multicultural Honor Award*

THE KIDS' MULTICULTURAL COOKBOOK
Food & Fun Around the World
by Deanna F. Cook

- *Parents' Choice Approved*
- *Parent's Guide Children's Media Award*

BOREDOM BUSTERS!
The Curious Kids' Activity Book
by Avery Hart and Paul Mantell

- *Parents' Choice Gold Award*
- *Benjamin Franklin Best Juvenile
  Nonfiction Award*

KIDS MAKE MUSIC!
Clapping and Tapping from Bach to Rock
by Avery Hart and Paul Mantell

HANDS AROUND THE WORLD
**365 Creative Ways to Build Cultural
Awareness & Global Respect**
by Susan Milord

- *Dr. Toy Best Vacation Product*
- *Parents' Choice Approved*

KIDS GARDEN!
**The Anytime, Anyplace Guide to Sowing &
Growing Fun**
by Avery Hart and Paul Mantell